YOU MUST BE BORN AGAIN

Tom Harmon

Ajoyin Publishing
P.O. Box 342, Three Rivers, MI 49093
888.273.4JOY
www.ajoyin.com

You Must Be Born Again

ISBN: 978-1-60920-015-2
Printed in the United States of America
©2011 by Tom Harmon
All rights reserved

Library of Congress Cataloging-in-Publication Data

Ajoyin Publishing, Inc.
P.O. 342
Three Rivers, MI 49093
www.ajoyin.com

First published 12/10/2008
978-1-4389-3703-8 (sc)

Please direct your inquiries to admin@ajoyin.com

Table of Contents

Foreword:

I want to leave a legacy of faith to my wife, children, grandchildren, and the people God brings within my sphere of influence. I hope that writing a series of books on consecrated living will aid me in this endeavor as well as strengthen my own faith.

Preface:

A consecrated life is one that is devoted to the worship and service of God. It is my personal belief that as a person grows in the grace and the knowledge of the Lord Jesus Christ, he develops an inner desire for consecrated living. Consecrated people still experience failure, but they have matured sufficiently to know how to trust God and benefit through their failures and continue on in their journey of faith. In Philippians 3:12, the Apostle Paul made it clear that he had not arrived at perfection: "Not as though I had already attained, either were already perfect; *but I follow after*, if that I may apprehend that for which also I am apprehended of Christ Jesus." As I attempt to write about the consecrated life, I will be writing from the perspective of one that is following after Christ Jesus, and not as one who has arrived.

Chapter 1:

The Gospel

I believe scripture indicates that it is possible to be "consecrated to God" in the sense of service and yet not be born again. Nicodemus is a classic example of this inconsistency. On the other hand many of the Epistles seem to indicate that it is also possible to be born again and not live a life of consecration to God. This is reflected in admonitions like "...put off the old man ... and ... put on the new man ..." (Col. 3:9-10), "walk not as other Gentiles walk, in the vanity of their mind" (Eph. 4:17), and "make no provision for the flesh, to fulfill its lust" (Rom. 13:14). It is in the process of experiencing God at work in us that we discover this inner desire to live a consecrated life from which people gain assurance of their salvation and appreciation for their faith relationship with the living Lord Jesus.

John 3:1-8: illustrates for us an example of a man who served God and yet was not born again.

"There was a man of the Pharisees, named Nicodemus, a ruler of the Jews; The same came to Jesus by night, and said unto him, Rabbi, we know that thou art a teacher come from God; for no man can do these miracles that thou doest, except God be with him. Jesus answered and said unto him, Verily, verily, I say unto thee, Except a man be born again, he cannot see the kingdom of God. Nicodemus saith unto him, How can a man be born when he is old? Can he enter the second time into his mother's womb, and be born? Jesus answered, Verily, verily, I say unto thee, Except a man be born of water and of the Spirit, he cannot enter into the kingdom of God. That which is born of the flesh is flesh; and that which is born of the Spirit is spirit. Marvel not that I say unto thee, Ye must be born again. The wind bloweth where it willeth, and thou hearest the sound of it, but canst not tell from where it cometh, and where it goeth; so is every one that is born of the Spirit."

Nicodemus was a highly religious man, living a life of service to God, very possibly doing many wonderful works in the name of Jehovah; yet Jesus made it very clear that at this point in the conversation, he was lost and in need of salvation. As of yet, he had not come to the truth of the gospel. A person cannot be born again until he hears the gospel. "How, then, shall they call on him in whom they have not believed? And how shall they believe in him of whom they have not heard? And how shall they hear without a preacher? And how shall they preach except they be sent? As it is written, How beautiful are the feet of them that who preach the gospel of peace, and bring glad tidings of good things!" (Rom. 10:14-15). The "good things" Paul is referring to have nothing to do with our good works, but only the good things of the Son of God. The gospel is focused solely on the person and work of Jesus Christ.

When the truth of the gospel is preached, and the Holy Spirit brings the necessary revelation of the truth of the gospel, a person can then be born again. "But God hath revealed them unto us by his Spirit; for the Spirit searcheth all things, yea the deep things of God. For what man knoweth the things of a man, except the spirit of a man which is in him? Even so the things of God knoweth no man, but the Spirit of God" (I Cor. 2:10-11). It is also the Holy Spirit who does the work of regeneration in giving the person new life, the new birth. "Not by works of righteousness which we have done, but according to his mercy he hath saved us, by the washing of regeneration, and the renewing of the Holy Spirit" (Titus 3:5). At this point the Holy Spirit enters the body of the believer and is joined to the human spirit. "But he that is joined unto the Lord is one spirit... What? Know ye not that your body is the temple of the Holy Spirit who is in you, whom ye have of God, and ye are not your own?"(I Cor. 6:17, 19). If a person has the Spirit of God living in them, they are born again, regardless of whether they are living a consecrated life or not. If a person is living a life of service for God and doing all the consecrated living they can, but does not have the Spirit of God living in them they are lost and still abiding under the wrath of God. "But ye are not in the flesh but in the Spirit, if so be the Spirit of God dwell in you. Now if any man have not the Spirit of Christ, he is none of his" (Rom. 8:9). What makes the difference in a lost person and a saved person is the Spirit of God.

Before presenting the gospel, I would like to share two things that have become precious to me in my personal embrace of the gospel.

Number one: Repentance and faith are necessary for true conversion and rebirth by the Spirit. When a person embraces repentance and faith, it is truly the grace of God at work, for on our best day, we could not genuinely produce these spiritual commodities. "For by grace are ye saved through faith; and that not of yourselves, it is the gift of God, not of works, lest any man should boast" (Eph. 2:8-9). Saving faith is a gift of grace. We also could not manufacture genuine repentance, "Or despisest thou the riches of his goodness and forbearance and long-suffering, not knowing that the goodness of God leadeth thee to repentance?" (Rom. 2:4). No man blazes his own trail to repentance; he is led there through the goodness and grace of Almighty God. Rom. 8:14: "For as many as are led by the Spirit of God, they are the sons of God." When a man turns away from his natural desire to be independent from God, it is due only to the work of Gods grace in his life.

Number two: One cannot be born again without the personal call of God to salvation. "Who hath saved us and called us with a holy calling, not according to our works, but according to his own purpose and grace, which was given us in Christ Jesus before the world began" (II Tim. 1:9). "But when it pleased God who separated me from my mother's womb, and called me by his grace, to reveal his son in me, that I might preach him among the Gentiles..." (Gal. 1:15-16). "God is faithful, by whom ye were called unto the fellowship of his son, Jesus Christ our Lord" (I Cor. 1:9). It is God who calls a man out of his dead, dark, lost condition, into God's marvelous light of eternal life. Salvation is of the Lord, and my call to him for salvation was not at my initiative, but in response to his call to me.

THE POWER OF THE GOSPEL IS IN THE GOSPEL

The gospel is not salvation: salvation is what occurs when the gospel is believed, but the gospel is the gospel whether it's believed or not. The gospel is good news, and what makes it good news is to know how bad the bad news is. The bad news is that we are born into life under the curse of the law—the law of God that demands perfection. The good news is that "Christ hath redeemed us from the curse of the law being made a curse for us" (Gal. 3:13a). The bad news is that all men are born in darkness, and it is from darkness that God calls us into light. "But you are a chosen generation, a royal priesthood, an holy nation, a people of his own, that ye should show forth the praises of him who hath called you out of darkness into his marvelous light" (I Pet. 2:9). So few of us really marvel at the light because we forget how dark our darkness really is.

My human nature is a nature of sin. By nature, I am opposed to God and his authority over me. By nature, I love to sin, then call it good so as to justify my sin, John 3:19: "And this is the condemnation, that light is come into the world, and men loved darkness rather than light, because their deeds were evil." Part of the nature of sin is an unwillingness to admit or even remotely acknowledge my love of sin. My willing ignorance of the capacity of sin hinders me all throughout my journey of faith. It feeds the Pharisee in me that claims to have some human capacity for walking out of the darkness on my own. Rather than admitting my blindness and receiving sight from God, I want to say I can see on my own, which only results in my remaining blind. "And Jesus said, for judgment I am come into this world, that they who see not might see; and that they who see, might be made blind. And some of the Pharisees who were with him heard these words, and said unto him, are we blind also? Jesus said unto them, if ye were blind, ye should have no sin. But now ye say, we see, therefore, your sin remaineth" (John 9:39-41). But, blessed be God, Jesus Christ came into the world to save sinners, of whom I am chief.

The simple gospel is this. "Therefore as by the offense of one the judgment came upon all men to condemnation, even so by the righteousness of one the free gift came upon all men unto justification of life" (Rom. 5:18). Another man's sin (Adam) made me a sinner, and another man's righteousness (Jesus) made me righteous. God's righteousness is the kind of righteousness that brings eternal life and the gift of salvation. It is not something we can work to attain; neither is it something we deserve. It is something that God in his mercy and grace gives to all those that believe. In Romans, chapter 4, Paul uses both Abraham and David as examples of men who understood the gift of God's imputed righteousness. "For what sayeth the Scriptures? Abraham believed God and it was counted to him for righteousness" (Rom. 4:3). "Even as David also describeth the blessedness of the man unto whom God imputeth righteousness apart from works, saying, blessed are they whose iniquities are forgiven, and whose sins are covered. Blessed is the man to whom the Lord will not impute sin" (Rom. 4:6-8).

A Twelve-year-old Theologian

A number of years ago, I was preaching to a group of about seventy-five junior high boys at Camp Barakel, one of my favorite camps, located in northern Michigan. It was a warm summer night, and we were around a campfire out in the national forest. There were mosquitoes and other distractions that often are a hindrance in preaching to boys of that age. During my message, I used the term *imputed righteousness*. They weren't listening all that well, and I knew I wasn't helping them with that kind of vocabulary. I asked if anyone knew what imputed righteousness meant, and a twelve-year-old boy shot his hand up, and everyone became instantly quiet. I didn't know it, but we were about to experience a "holy moment." The young man said with distinct clarity, "Imputed righteousness is when Jesus died on the cross, all my sin was imputed, or put upon him. And when I by faith received Christ as my savior, all his righteousness was imputed or put upon me." There was a holy hush over the entire group as his proclamation swept over all of us. You can have your PhD in theology and not be able to give a more accurate or concise definition of imputed righteousness, which is the good news of the gospel. I also remembered that Jesus was twelve years old when he was in the temple giving answers to the PhDs of his day. I've since been more respectful of twelve-year-old theologians.

Salvation through the gospel is "To declare, I say, at this time his righteousness, that he might be just and the justifier of him who believeth in Jesus" (Rom. 3:26). It's when we stop striving to save ourselves and come to rest in the finished work of the cross and his imputed righteousness that "But to him that worketh not but believeth on him that justifieth the ungodly, his faith is counted for righteousness" (Rom. 4:5). Once again, another man's sin (Adam) made me a sinner, and another man's righteousness (Jesus) has made me righteous. When a person senses the call of God to salvation through the only way God has provided John 17:3: "And this is life eternal, that they may know thee, the only true God, and his son Jesus Christ, whom thou hast sent" when they sense God leading them to repentance and faith— that is, from being independent of God to being totally dependent on God. God puts his Spirit in them and they become a new creation. The transaction is complete: you are born again, a new creation; "old things are passed away, and behold, all things are become new" (II Cor. 5:17). "He hath made him who knew no sin, to be sin for us, that we might be made the righteousness of God in him" (II Cor. 5:21).

For years, I struggled with assurance of my salvation. I looked at my life and wondered if I were truly born again. Some people go so far as to say that no one can really know for sure if they are truly born again. But the scriptures teach otherwise; I John 2:3: "And by this do we know that we know him, if we keep his commandments." Also in I John 5:13-15: "These things have I written unto you that believe on the name of the Son of God, that ye may know that ye have eternal life, And this is the confidence that we have in him that if we ask anything according to his will, he heareth us; and we know that if he hear us, whatever we ask, we know that we have the petitions that we desired of him."

In John 4, Jesus asked a woman for a drink of water. She responded in shock that he would ask her, for he was a Jew and she was a Samaritan, and the Jews had no dealings with the Samaritans. Jesus said to her, If you only knew who it is that asketh you a drink of water, you would ask me for a drink and I would give you living water. Jesus went on to tell her that the water from the town well would only make her thirst again, but the water he would give her would become in her a well of water springing up into everlasting life. Later she did ask him for that water. When Jesus told her that he was the water, she believed him and received exactly what Jesus had promised, eternal life. Salvation is as simple as falling off a log if God is in it, and it is impossible if He's not in it. The disciples learned this as the rich young ruler walked away and they said unto Jesus, "who then can be saved? But Jesus beheld them and said unto them, with men this is impossible, but with God all things are possible" (Matt. 19:26).

CHAPTER 2:

SEEING YOURSELF A SINNER

While most people would agree that nobody's perfect, very few are willing to admit we possess the same capacity for evil as Satan himself. It's hard to imagine the Apostle Paul could be describing the entire human race in Romans 1:28-31, when he says we are "filled with all unrighteousness, fornication, wickedness, covetousness, maliciousness, full of envy, murder, strife, deceit, malignity, whisperers, backbiters, haters of God, insolent, proud, boasters, inventors of evil things, disobedient to parents, without understanding, covenant breakers, without natural affection, implacable, unmerciful." Because of these things, Romans 5:10 describes the condition of our natural birth and refers to us as enemies of God. Ephesians 2:3 says that our very nature is opposed to the God who created us. Colossians 1:21 says that we are described as being alienated and enemies in our mind by wicked works (Col. 1:21). The horrible sin of pride doesn't want me to see myself in this light. The sin of self-righteousness wants me to think better of myself than I really am. In Job 1:8, God said that there was none as good as Job; not in all the earth could a man be found as upright as he. Yet in Job 9:21, Job said, "If I justify myself, my own mouth will condemn me; if I say I am perfect, he shall also prove me perverse." Find the best man going, and in him you will find a sinner, capable of the most horrible depravity.

What Is Sin?

Sin can be as simple as knowing the right thing to do and not doing it. James 4:17: "To him that knoweth to do good and doeth it not, to him it is sin." Sin can be flat-out rebellion against God's law. I John 3:4: "Whosoever committeth sin transgresseth also the law; for sin is the transgression of the law." Sin is a relentless force within us, providing an endless supply of thoughts and actions contrary to the nature and character of the holy God who created us. Genesis 6:3: "And God saw that the wickedness of man was great in the earth and that every imagination of the thoughts of his heart was only evil continually." Oftentimes we hate the consequences of sin and yet are driven by sin that we may enjoy the short-lived pleasures it affords. In Hebrews 11:25, it is said of Moses that he chose rather to suffer the affliction with the people of God than to enjoy the pleasures of sin for a season. Sin is many things, but most of all, it is deceitful. This deceit lives within the dim regions of our darkened hearts. It hardens our hearts, deafens our ears, and blinds our eyes from seeing ourselves the sinners we truly are. It is only the loving mercy of God that reveals this truth to us, for without it, we will trust in some self-imposed standard of our own goodness. " For there is not a just man upon the earth, that doeth good and sinneth not" (Ecc. 7:20). It is only by the mercy of God that we can glimpse the awful state of our sin, and it's only by the grace of God that we can turn to Christ for complete forgiveness. "In whom we have redemption thorough his blood, the forgiveness of sins, according to the riches of his grace" (Eph. 1:7).

No One Knew Sin Better Than Jesus

Though Jesus knew sin better than anyone, he himself was without sin. Hebrews 4:15: says He "was in all points tempted like as we are, yet without sin." "Who did no sin, neither was guile found in his mouth" (I Pet. 2:22). Because Jesus was sinless, he is the only credible authority to speak on it. The apostle John records a powerful insight in the gospel of John 2:23-25: "Now when he was in Jerusalem at the Passover, in the feast day, many believed in his name when they saw the miracles which he did. But Jesus did not commit himself unto them, *because he knew all men*. And needed not that any should testify of man, *for he knew what was in man*."

Jesus Knew The Very Heart Of Man

In Mark 7, the Pharisees accused the disciples of being defiled because they forgot to wash their hands before they ate. The disciples of Jesus were defiled, all right, but not because of what went into them, but because of what was already there. Jesus made it clear that nothing from outside of a man entering into him can defile him, but the things which come out of him, those are what defile the man. In Mark 7:21-23, Jesus makes it clear what is in man: "For from within, out of the heart of men, proceed evil thoughts, adulteries, fornications, murders, thefts, covetousness, wickedness, deceit, lasciviousness, an evil eye, blasphemy, pride, foolishness." All these things come from within, and defile the man.

The Deeper A Man Sees The Pit Of His Sin, The Firmer He Will Stand On The Rock Of His Salvation.

When a man truly understands his sinful state he's more apt to keep going in the right ways of God than to return to the sinful ways of himself, for those are the ways of the miry clay. I don't think it is possible for a man to have a genuine and sincere love for God without a genuine and sincere brokenness over the depth of his sin. I don't think it is possible to marvel over the greatness of your salvation without seeing how hopeless you are in your sin. "But ye are a chosen generation, a royal priesthood, an holy nation, a people of his own, that you should show forth the praises of him who hath called you out of darkness into his marvelous light; who in time past were not a people, but now are the people of God; who had not obtained mercy but now have obtained mercy" (I Pet. 2:9-10).

In John, chapter 3, we hear the story of a man named Nicodemus. He was a Pharisee and a religious teacher of the Jews. The description of the heart of man given by Jesus in Mark 7:21-22 surely didn't apply to him. Other men may have hearts that contain such horrible things, but not his. Luke 18:9-14 shows how strongly the Pharisees opposed the teaching of Jesus on man's sinfulness:

> And he spoke this parable unto certain who trusted in themselves that they were righteous, and despised others: Two men went up into the temple to pray; the one was a Pharisee, and the other was a tax collector. The Pharisee stood and prayed thus with himself, God, I thank thee that I am not as other men are, extortioners, unjust, adulterers, or even as this tax collector. I fast twice a week; I give tithes of all that I possess. And the tax collector,

standing afar off, would not lift up his eyes unto heaven, but smote upon his breast, saying, God, be merciful unto me, a sinner. I tell you this man went down to his house justified rather than the other; for everyone that exalteth himself shall be abased; and every one that humbleth himself shall be exalted.

A Man Cannot Be Justified In The Sight Of God Who Does Not See Himself A Sinner.

John 9 is the account of Jesus healing a man who was born blind. After some intense interrogation, the Pharisees threw this man out of the synagogue because he wouldn't call Jesus a sinner, but instead, he said, "If this man were not of God, he could do nothing." In verse 34, the Pharisees make a statement that reveals much of their theology: aiming at the man who had just been healed of his blindness, they said, "Thou wast altogether born in sins, and dost thou teach us?" And they cast him out. The Pharisees did not believe that Adam's one sin would make all of his descendents to be born in sin. "Therefore by the offence of one the judgment *came upon all men* unto condemnation" (Rom. 5:18). Romans 5:12 also makes it clear that sin entered the world through one man, and that man was the first man, Adam. Genesis 3:6 records the exact moment sin entered the world and captures it in these four words: "and he did eat." One seemingly small sin started an avalanche of destructive sins that man would never have had to know, but now we know them all too well.

It is truly humbling to view ourselves as totally depraved. This humility is a blessing from God and opens our eyes to God's only way of salvation. In John 14:6, Jesus said that he was the way the truth and the life, and no man could come to the Father but by him. Even after we come to Christ and are born again, sin still plays a hard hand against our following the ways of Christ. This old, indwelling sin will continue to oppose everything the new, divine nature wants me to do. Oh, yes, I am a new creation (II Cor. 5:17), yet sin still dwells in me. "Now, then, it is no more I that do it, but sin that dwelleth in me. For I know that in me (that is in my flesh) dwelleth no good thing; for to will is present with me, but how to perform that which is good I find not" (Rom. 7:17-18). A Christian will never find the power to live the Christian life when looking in the wrong place, and looking to yourself is the wrong place. Hebrews 12:2 is the only right place: "Looking unto Jesus, the author and finisher of our faith."

In most of Paul's letters, he warned the saints of the dangers of sin. "For I say through the grace given unto me, to every man that is among you, not to think of himself more highly than he ought to think, but to think soberly, according as God hath dealt to every man the measure of faith" (Rom. 12:3). If I am to avoid the trap of thinking to highly of myself, I must learn to view myself correctly (biblically). One who views himself a sinner with a capacity for horrible depravity is less likely to become self-sufficient. "Not that we are sufficient of ourselves to think anything of ourselves, but our sufficiency is of God" (II Cor. 3:5). "For if a man think himself to be something, when he is nothing, he deceiveth himself" (Gal. 6:3). The Apostle Paul demonstrated this for us in his writings; in I Corinthians 15:9, he stated that he was the least of the apostles because he persecuted the church of God. He may have viewed himself as the least of the apostles, but he still identified himself as part of that elite group of church leaders. Four years later, he wrote in Ephesians 3:8 that he was less than the least of all saints. Four years later, he wrote in I Timothy 1:15 that "Christ Jesus came into the world to save sinners of whom I am chief." It is clear from Romans 7 that Paul knew that sin dwelt in him and that in his flesh dwelt no good thing. No wonder he would cry out, "Oh, wretched man that *I am*"—notice he didn't say, "Oh, wretched man that I was." Paul knew well the nature of sin and the sin that lived in his flesh would love to show itself if given the slightest opportunity.

Few Old Men Finish Well

Scripture records that few old men finish well, even the "greats." Men who truly knew the Lord and experienced his grace in their lives did not finish well. For example, Noah, after years of building the ark, being a preacher of righteousness, and witnessing firsthand God's salvation on the ark. Noah plants a vineyard, harvests the grapes, makes the wine, gets drunk, gets naked, and curses his son (Gen. 9:20-23). Samson is a man who experienced the Spirit of the Lord upon him in feats of physical strength like no other man. He was an absolute moral failure and died suicidal among the enemies he was supposed to have conquered (Judges 16:30). King Saul in his final days found himself so far from the Lord that he stooped to consulting a witch (I Sam. 28:7). Near the end of David's life, he began to drift from his confidence in the Almighty as his deliverer. Earlier in his life, he wrote in Psalms 20:7, "Some trust in chariots, and some in horses, but we will remember the name of the Lord our God." He had always known that the outcome of the battle didn't depend on the number of his soldiers. Yet his sin of numbering the strength of his army cost the lives of seventy thousand men from Dan to Beer-Sheba (II Sam. 24:15). The wisest man who ever lived, Solomon, died a babbling old fool worshiping idols in the temples of his foreign wives, and God was not pleased with him.

The Apostle Paul finished well. "I have fought a good fight, I have finished my course, I have kept the faith" (II Tim 4:7). I wonder how much Paul's understanding of the nature of sin and his own capacity for depravity contributed to his success. I think the following verses reflect some of his understanding. Wherefore, let him who thinketh he standeth take heed lest he fall" (I Cor. 10:12). "Brethren, if a man be overtaken in a fault, ye who are spiritual restore such a one in the spirit of meekness, considering thyself, lest thou also be tempted" (Gal. 6:1). "For I know that in me, (that is, in my flesh) dwelleth no good thing; for to will is present with me; but how to perform that which is good I find not"(Rom 7:18). "Oh, wretched man that I am! Who shall deliver me from the body of this death?" (Rom. 7:24).

I've just read the things I have written, and though I believe every word I've put down, I must admit it paints man as a pretty hopeless case, but that's exactly what a man is without Christ. "That at that time ye were without Christ, being aliens from the commonwealth of Israel, and strangers from the covenants of promise, having no hope, and without God in the world" (Eph 2:12). Sin is a powerful force within that drives us to godless behavior. Unless a man can see the depth of his sin, he will never see his desperate need for God's mercy and salvation. I've found the more I understand the horrors of my sin, the more I appreciate the love of God. Without seeing myself in total depravity, I will not understand why I still struggle with sin even after I have received God's forgiveness and received the Holy Spirit and the gift of salvation. If I am ever to gain victory over trusting in myself rather than the living God, it must come as a result of a well-cultivated understanding of my total depravity. From this position, we begin to gain an appreciation for the cross of Jesus Christ. From this position, we begin to see the need for daily application of the truth of the cross, and what was really accomplished there. The nature of sin, the nature of man, the nature of Satan—these three are one, and they all blind us from seeing the hope we have in the finished work of Jesus Christ at Calvary.

Chapter 3:

What Does It Take to Be Born Again?

John chapter 3 gives an explicitly detailed account of Nicodemus's encounter with Jesus. Nicodemus was a man, and as such, he was totally depraved, regardless of how much religion he had. Depravity can hide very well when clothed in religious ritual. His depravity was well hidden, even from himself. This religiously lost man sincerely believed, and verbally confessed, that Jesus was a man come from God. Nicodemus had seen the miracles, and he knew the Jehovah God must be with Jesus. In verse 3 Jesus said, "Except a man be born again, he cannot see the kingdom of God."

At the risk of sounding foolish, Nicodemus asked, "How can a man be born when he old? Can he enter the second time into his mother's womb and be born?"

Jesus gave him the truth, and said again, "Except a man be born of water and of the Spirit, he cannot enter the kingdom of God. That which is born of the flesh is flesh, and that which is born of the Spirit is spirit. Marvel not that I say unto you, you must be born again." Remember that Nicodemus has just confessed that Jesus is a teacher come from God. Now, Nicodemus hears Jesus say that in his present condition, Nicodemus would not enter the kingdom of God. No news could have rocked him more.

Jesus mentions two things that are necessary in order to be born again: they are water and the Spirit. Failure to be born again means you cannot enter the kingdom of God, and Nicodemus is not born again.

Question; What does it mean to be born of water? Some Bible commentators say this is referring to our natural birth, because we were contained in a sack of amniotic fluid just prior to natural birth. Some think this is referring to water baptism. My belief is that Jesus is using the word "water" metaphorically to symbolize the Word of God. There are many word pictures used to illustrate important characteristics of the Scriptures. In I Peter 2:2, the word of God is referred to as *milk*; in Matthew 4:4, it's referred to as *bread*; in Luke 8:11, it's referred to as the *seed*; in Psalms 119:105, it's referred to as a *lamp* and a *light*. "Is not my word like a fire saith the Lord; and like a hammer that breaketh the rock in pieces" (Jer. 23:29). In Ephesians 5:26, husbands are told to sanctify and cleanse their wives by the washing of *water by the word.* "Being *born again*, not of corruptible *seed*, but of incorruptible, *by the word of God*, which liveth and abideth forever" (I Pet 1:23). Can someone be born again who has never heard the word of God? "How, then, shall they call on him in whom they have not believed? How shall they believe in him of whom they have not heard? And how shall they hear without a preacher? And how shall they preach, except they be sent?" (Rom. 10:14-15a).

Is It Possible To Hear The Word Of God And Believe It And Not Be Born Again?

I asked myself the question, is it possible to hear the word of God and believe it and yet not be born again? As I sat in my study and pondered that question, three people quickly came to mind. All of them grew up in Christian homes, attended Bible believing churches, and had at one time or another made a profession of faith in Jesus as their savior. All of them during their mid to late teens had bolted away from their upbringing and began to live void of any relationship with Christ. One stole money from his parents and ran away for months. He seemed determined to go his own way. He later wrote me a letter explaining that he had heard the gospel all his life and believed that he had believed it. He had even been told that he had believed it, but was not born again. He has now been born again, and his life bears evidence of the new creation. The second young man was very similar. He grew up on the mission field with Christian parents, having heard the gospel all his life. He also believed that he believed and was told that he believed. In his late teens, he also bolted and lacked any evidence of the indwelling Spirit of God. In his own testimony, he said that he was not born again. Today, he is a pastor, with a passion for the gospel and a genuine heart for the religiously lost. The third young man was very similar: Christian home, Bible preaching church, Christian school graduate, and also believed that he believed and was told that he believed, but was not born again. He got involved in hard drugs, crime, and immorality and seemed unrestrained in his attempts to destroy his life. There was no evidence of Christ in his life. In his own testimony, he admits that he was not born again. He now has a life that bears evidence of a relationship with God. God has supernaturally freed him from drugs, which is not to be misinterpreted that he no longer has any problems, but that he now has a "new man" that has access to everything he needs for life and godliness. *Being born again is a relationship with God through faith in his son Jesus Christ.* This will be explained further in Chapter four.

Nicodemus Was A Classic Example Of Hearing And Believing

Nicodemus had heard the word of God and believed it. He was a teacher of the Jews and believed in all the

Old Testament scriptures and yet confessed in verse 9 that he didn't understand these things. In verse 10, Jesus wondered at how he could teach scriptures in Israel and not understand these things. This wasn't some new doctrine or new gospel that Jesus was teaching. In John 5:39, Jesus rebukes the Pharisees for their approach to scriptures: "Search the scriptures; for in them ye think ye have eternal life; and they are they which testify of me. And ye will not come to me that ye might have life." It is sobering to think a person can have the scripture, even be a teacher of scripture and think he is born again, when he isn't.

The scriptures testify of Christ, beginning with Moses and all of the prophets (Acts 24:27), yet they wouldn't come to him that they might have life. John 6:44: "No man can come to me, except the Father who sent me draw him." Could it be they were hardened to the work of God's Spirit? "Wherefore, as the Holy Spirit saith, Today if you will hear his voice, harden not your hearts" (Heb. 3:7-8). Could it be they were quenching the work of God's Spirit? "Quench not the Spirit" (I Thess. 5:19). Could it be they were resisting the work of God's Spirit? "Ye stiff-necked and uncircumcised in heart and ears, ye do always resist the Holy Spirit; as your fathers did, so do ye" (Acts 7:51).

Is God At Work In People's Lives, Yet They Lack The Gospel?

Is it possible to have God at work in your life, and yet not become born again because you lack the truth of the knowledge of Christ? Is it possible to have a divine healing and yet not be born again? In John, chapter 9, Jesus heals a man born blind. The healed man testifies in verse 33, "If this man [Jesus] were not of God he could do nothing." The Pharisees cast the healed man out of the temple. Jesus found him and asked him if he believed on the Son of God. The man said, "Who is he, sir, that I might believe on him?" "And Jesus said unto him, thou hast both seen him, and it is he that talketh with thee" (37). The man said, "Lord, I believe. And he worshiped him" (38) at that point he was born again.

In Acts 10, Cornelius, a centurion of the Italian band, had grown weary of the gods of Rome. He had become quite devout to the one God of the Jews, giving alms, saying prayers, and had developed a genuine fear of God. An angel of God appeared in a vision and told him to send to Joppa for a man named Peter who would come and tell him what he needed to do. You may wonder why God didn't just have the angel tell Cornelius the word of the gospel. God, in his sovereign omniscience, has chosen to use people to be the vehicle through which the message is shared. At the same time, God was working in Peter's life to prepare him to take the gospel message to the Gentiles. When Peter arrived and preached the gospel, the Holy Spirit came upon the listeners, and they were born again. There is a need for both the word of God and the Spirit of God in order for a person to be born again. "That which is born of the flesh is flesh, and that which is born of the Spirit is spirit."

Is It Possible To Have The Gospel Preached, The Holy Spirit At Work, And A Person Still Not Be Born Again?

Is it possible to have the gospel preached and the Spirit of God working in conviction and leading to repentance and for the person still not to be born again? It seems that was the case in at least two instances. One such instance is recorded in Acts 24, when the Apostle Paul is reasoning with Felix of righteousness, temperance, and of judgment to come. In verse 25, it says that Felix trembled, yet nowhere does it say he believed and was born again. In Acts 26, Paul shares his testimony and powerfully presents the gospel before Agrippa and a panel of political dignitaries. The haunting response of Agrippa is recorded for eternity: "Almost thou persuadest me to be a Christian" (Acts 26:28).

It would seem from John, chapter 3, that the word of the gospel and the work of God's spirit are both necessary ingredients in the new birth. If the hearer responds in the grace and faith given to him by God at that moment, he is born of the Spirit. If not, he remains in his sin. I must confess there is some mystery in all of this. It may be that God intended it to remain so, for Jesus goes on to say to Nicodemus in verse 8, "The wind bloweth where it willeth, and thou hearest the sound of it, but canst not tell from where it cometh or where it goeth; so is everyone that is born of the Spirit." I know I have heard and understood the word of the gospel. I know the Spirit of God has convicted me of my sin and given me grace and faith to receive Christ as my savior. The difficult part of all this is trying to understand why the wind blows upon anyone, why the wind blew on me, and why I breathed it in, and why I am a child of his sovereign grace. David said it so well in Psalms 8:3-4: "When I consider thy heavens, the works of thy fingers, the moon and the stars, which thou hast ordained, What is man, that thou art mindful of him? And the son of man, that thou visitest him?" God has surely done this for his glory. "That no flesh should glory in his presence. But of Him are ye in Christ Jesus, who of God is made unto us wisdom, and righteousness, and sanctification, and redemption; that, according as it is written, He that glorieth, let him glory in the Lord" (I Cor. 1:29).

Chapter 4:

What Does It Mean to Be Born Again?

"That which is born of the flesh is flesh; and that which is born of the Spirit is spirit" (John. 3:6). Salvation is a spiritual experience, and we must see ourselves as spiritual beings. Humanity often sees itself primarily as a physical being with some spiritual interests. The truth is, we are primarily spiritual beings with physical limitations. "For what man knoweth the things of a man, except the spirit of a man which is in him?" (I Cor. 2:11). Man also has a soul. The soul of man is distinguishable from his spirit, yet inseparably linked to his spirit. "And the very God of peace sanctify you wholly; and I pray God your whole spirit and soul, and body be preserved blameless unto the coming of our Lord Jesus Christ." (1 Thess. 5:23). The Greek word for *spirit* in this verse is *pneuma,* and it means *current of air, breath,* or *breeze.* Man's breath is his most urgent need to sustain life. The Greek word for *soul* is *psuche,* where we get our English word for psyche or the mind, will, and emotions. The Greek word for *body* is *soma* which is made up of flesh and bones. In order to explain salvation and best understand what it means to be born again, **we need to see ourselves as a spirit, in a body, with a soul.** "And the Lord God formed man of the dust of the ground [body], and breathed into his nostrils the breath of life [spirit]; and man became a living soul" (Gen. 2:7).

MAN IS A SPIRIT IN A BODY WITH A SOUL

The Lord Jesus had a body. "Who his own self bore our sins in his own body on the tree..." (1 Pet. 2:24). At the death of Jesus, Joseph of Arimathaea went to Pilate and begged the body of Jesus that he might bury it in the tomb he had prepared for himself (Matt. 27:57-58). Jesus had a soul. As Jesus and his disciples were in Gethsemane, he said to Peter, James, and John, "My soul is exceedingly sorrowful, even unto death; tarry here, and watch with me" (Matt. 26:38). In Luke 23:46, His last words are recorded as being, "Father into thy hands I commend my spirit, and, having said this, he gave up the spirit."

Mary, the mother of the Lord Jesus, also was a spirit in a body with a soul. Jesus was carried in her womb and made of her body. "But, when the fullness of time was come, God sent forth his Son, made of a woman, made under the law" (Gal. 4:4). Mary had a soul. "And Mary said my soul doth magnify the Lord" (Luke 1:46). She had a spirit. "And my spirit hath rejoiced in God my savior" (Luke 1:47).

The spirit is reborn, not the soul or the body. Jesus said that which is born of the Spirit is spirit. Wouldn't it be wonderful if at the moment of salvation, we received our resurrected body that could travel as fast as thought (Luke 24:31), enter a room while the doors are shut (John 20:19), eat food but not have to eat it to live (Luke 24:43)? It would be wonderful, all right, but that's just not the way it is. Oh, the day is coming, bless God, when our bodies will be redeemed from the bondage of corruption. Yes, the whole of creation groaneth and travaileth in pain together until now waiting for the day when we get our new bodies (Rom. 8:21-23). Our immortal, reborn spirits remain in our mortal bodies (Rom. 6:12). The body of a born-again person continues to die because the curse of sin still dwells in it (Rom. 6:13). Yet we have this promise that one day, Jesus will appear, and we shall be like Him, for we shall see Him as He is, and the dead shall be raised incorruptible and we shall be changed, for this corruptible must put on incorruption, and this mortal must put on immortality (I John 3:2 and I Cor. 15:53).

Was Jesus mortal? The Bible is clear that the wages of sin is death (Rom. 6:23). We know that Jesus was tempted in all points like we are yet without sin (Heb. 4:15). Though Jesus was immortal, the body of Jesus became mortal when God the Father made him become sin for us. "For He hath made Him, who knew no sin, to be sin for us, that we might be made the righteousness of God in Him." (II Cor. 5:21). The condemnation of Adam's sin has passed on to all of us from our earthly father. God the father sent his son Jesus in the likeness of sinful flesh and for sin and condemned sin in the flesh (Rom. 8:3). In the love and mercy of God, Jesus was made mortal to pay the price of our sin.

Was Jesus born twice? We know from Luke 2:11 that Jesus was born once: "For unto you is born this day in the city of David a savior, who is Christ the Lord." But was Jesus born a second time? "Christ is the head of the body, the church, who is the beginning, the first born from the dead, that in all things he might have the pre-eminence" (Col. 1:18). It was God's intent that Jesus should be the first one to have a resurrected body; the first one to be reborn in body by the Spirit. "For Christ also hath once suffered for sins, the just for the unjust, that he might bring us to God, being put to death in the flesh but made alive by the Spirit" (I Pet. 3:18).

If the Spirit of God thought it important to redeem Jesus' body surely he has an interest in our bodies, yet not to the exclusion of our spirits. Because the body is created by God, we should be responsible in taking care of it. We should eat right, get the proper amount of rest, exercise, etc. "For bodily exercise profiteth little, but godliness is profitable unto all things, having promise of the life that now is and of that which is to come" (1 Tim. 4:8) We live in a culture that has become obsessed with the body to the neglect of what's inside the body, our spirit. Today, you can have your fat or your wrinkles removed, or both. You can have your nose made smaller, your ears trimmed, teeth straightened, chin shrunk, lips enlarged, or whatever your fancy may be, and not be one bit closer to being born again.

The spirit is born again, not the soul. Wouldn't it be wonderful if, as soon as a person was born again, they never had a sinful word come out of their mouth, never had a sinful thought in their mind, never felt sinful feelings of any kind? If that were true once a person was born again they would never have a sinful action of any kind. This is simply not so. Oh, yes, we now have the mind of Christ (I Cor. 2:16), but we are to let this mind be in us as was also in Christ Jesus (Phil. 2:5). The divine nature that we are partakers of (II Pet. 1:4) is up against the nature of sin that still has access to our soul, the way we think, act, and feel. We are to put off this old man and put on the new (Col. 3:9-10). This is what is referred to as the conversion of our soul, which is the subject matter for chapter five.

What does it mean to be born again? "And you hath he made alive who were dead in trespasses and sins" (Eph. 2:1). What does this mean? In what way were we dead? We weren't dead physically or mentally or emotionally. Though our human spirit was alive within us, we were spiritually dead. We had no fellowship with the Lord God who made us. The living has no fellowship with the dead.

When a dead person is placed in a grave, he is laid out in a horizontal position. The spirit of a man is in a horizontal position prior to being born of the Spirit. He is physically alive, mentally and emotionally alive. His soul is alive and can make decisions and respond to things he hears and sees, yet he is spiritually dead. When a person hears the word of the gospel, the Holy Spirit begins to breathe life into the dead spirit through the soul. The Holy Spirit begins to give grace and faith, and the spirit of the person who was dead in trespasses and sins comes to life and rises up in a vertical position and is joined with the Holy Spirit within the person's body (I Cor. 6:17, 19). This joining together is as intimate as marriage, and two become one spirit in the Lord.

"And the Lord God took the man and put him into the garden of Eden to till it and keep it. And the Lord God commanded the man, saying, Of every tree of the garden, thou mayest freely eat; But of the tree of the knowledge of good and evil, thou shalt not eat of it; for in the day that thou eatest thereof thou shalt surely die" (Gen. 2:15-17). Both Adam and Eve ate, but neither of them died that day, or did they? We know they didn't die physically on that day; they didn't die mentally or emotionally. They both were capable of making decisions: they hid themselves; they made aprons of fig leaves to cover their nakedness. They had been spiritually alive and able to fellowship with God, who is a spirit. Though their spirits were giving life to their bodies, they were spiritually dead in their trespasses and sins. "God, who is rich in mercy, for his great love with which he loved them" (Eph. 2:4), began to access their spiritual deadness through their souls. He led them to repentance through a series of self-examination questions (Gen 2:9-13). He placed a curse on the serpent, and in the same breath made a promise to put enmity between the serpent and the seed of the woman. Satan would bruise the woman's seed, but in the end, the woman's seed would crush Satan's head (Gen. 3:14-15). Adam knew his sin would affect him all the days of his life, but he believed God's promise of life, and as an expression of his faith, he renamed his wife Eve, the mother of all living. And God made them coats of skins and clothed them, and once again, they were spiritually alive. Everything had changed in their bodies and souls, but spiritually, they were a new creation and once again alive and one with God in the spirit.

You Must Be Born Again

The born-again experience is a must. Jesus made that clear to Nicodemus in John 3:7: "Marvel not that I say unto *you, you must* be born again." Just as one must have air to live, one must be born again to enter the kingdom of God. It is impossible to live without oxygen, and it is impossible to go to heaven without being born of the Spirit of God. "And as Moses lifted up the serpent in the wilderness, even so *must* the Son of man be lifted up" (John 3:14). "And he began to teach them that the Son of man *must* suffer many things, and to be rejected by the elders, and by the chief priests, and the scribes, and be killed, and after three days rise again" (Mark 8:31). "For as yet they knew not the scripture, that he *must* rise again from the dead" (John 20:9). From the suffering of Christ, to his crucifixion and resurrection, all *must* be fulfilled in order for us to have our sins forgiven and be born again" In Acts 16:30, the Philippian jailer cried out to Paul, "What *must* I do to be saved?" Paul's answer was clear and to the point: "Believe on the Lord Jesus Christ and thou shalt be saved." Paul was not saying, "Just put Jesus on the shelf to compete with all the other gods of this world," but that there was only one God and one mediator between God and men, the man Christ Jesus (I Tim. 2:5). The words of Paul and the work of the Holy Spirit brought life to Acts 4:12: "Neither is there salvation in any other; for there is no other name under heaven given among men whereby we *must* be saved." The jailer rejoiced and believed with all his house (Acts 16:34).

CHAPTER 5:

CONVERTING THE SOUL

The most basic definition for the word *convert* is to undergo a change. The moment a person is born again he goes through a complete identity change, i.e. from being dead in sins to being made alive in Christ (Eph. 2:1, 5), from being an enemy of God (Rom. 5:10) to being made a friend of God (John 15:15), from being under the curse of the law (Gal. 3:13) to having every spiritual blessing in heavenly places in Christ Jesus (Eph. 1:3), from being condemned (John 3:18) to being justified (Rom. 5:1). When my spirit is born of the Spirit of God, the change is complete. "And ye are complete in Him, who is the head of all principalities and power" (Col. 2:10). I am totally accepted in the beloved (Eph. 1:6), and my status has changed from being a child of the devil (John 8:44) to being a child of the living God (John 1:12). I have a whole new position spiritually, and it's not because of my family bloodlines; it's not because of some will of my own or some self-manufactured determination of my own. It is only the Spirit of God who accomplishes all these identity changes in my spirit.

It Is The Spirit That Is Born Again, Not The Body Or The Soul

It is the spirit that is born again, not the soul or the body. The soul and the spirit are inseparable, yet distinguishable. "Therefore if any man be in Christ, he is a new creation; old things are passed away; behold, all things are become new" (II Cor. 5:17). The spirit part of me is what this verse is referring to, not the soul. We know our bodies remain under the curse of sin and death after we are born again. Though we may have a new capacity for health and wellness because of the work of Christ in our souls, we do not get our new bodies until the day of resurrection when Christ redeems our bodies, which is his purchased possession (Eph. 1:14).

The soul is made up of our intellect, emotions, and will. When a person is born of the Spirit, his soul continues to have many of the old thought patterns and old feelings, and thus, many of the old actions. The change in my spirit was made instantly. The conversion of my soul is a process that will go on throughout my life. "Brethren, if any of you do err from the truth, and one convert him, let him know that he who converteth the sinner from the error of his way shall save a soul from death, and shall hide a multitude of sins" (James 5:19-20). According to this passage, Christians can err from living according to God's word. Their souls can persist in sinning, and fellowship with God is broken. The brother in the Lord who sees this and comes alongside the one who is in error and speaks the truth in love, prays for him, and does whatever he can do to convert (help him change) will protect him from a multitude of sins that would only draw him farther away from God. He saves his soul from death, or the inability to produce any spiritual fruit.

How Do You Engraft The Word Into Your Life And Have It Save Your Soul?

Wherefore, put away all filthiness and overflowing of wickedness, and receive with meekness the engrafted word, which is able to save your souls" (James 1:21). "The law of the Lord is perfect, converting the soul; the testimony of the Lord is sure, making wise the simple" (Ps. 19:7). How do you engraft the word into your life and have it save your soul? Whoso keepeth his mouth and his tongue, keepeth his soul from troubles" (Prov. 21:23). If I receive that truth and meditate on it, eventually, the opportunity will come, and the Holy Spirit will prompt me to obey. The more I obey the voice of God, the weaker the flesh becomes, and all the while I grow stronger in the spirit. This process is called the conversion of my soul. I have seen the blessings that come from keeping my mouth shut when God tells me to. There have been times when I have disobeyed God, shot off my mouth when I knew he was telling me to be quiet, and regretted it. I have lain awake nights worrying over things I've said. I have made myself sick and been miserable in my soul because of not listening to the Spirit of God and obeying him when he was telling me to keep still.

One of the truly great evidences that you are born again is that God's spirit will speak to your spirit that you are a child of God (Rom. 8:16). God went through your soul (mind, will, emotions) to bring about conviction to your spirit, as we saw in the case of Adam. In His goodness He led our souls to repentance. "Or despisest thou the riches of his goodness and forbearance and longsuffering, not knowing that the goodness of God leadeth thee to repentance?" (Rom. 2:4). We did not blaze our own trail to repentance, for we were spiritually dead when God began to minister to our minds, wills, and emotions. When a person is born again, God now speaks to the spirit, and this new man which is created after God in Christ (Eph. 4:24) will tell the soul, "There is a new master here, and his name is Jesus, and old soul, you are going to change." This kind of obedience can only come through the power of the Spirit. There is the new chain of command in the life of a born-again person: God's spirit speaking to our spirit, our spirit speaking to our soul, and our soul telling our body how to behave.

Peter speaks about our sanctification. "Elect according to the foreknowledge of God, the Father, *through sanctification of the Spirit,* unto obedience..." (I Pet. 1:2). If we can see ourselves as a spirit, in a body with a soul, it will give us another framework for understanding sanctification. "Seeing that ye have purified your souls in obeying the truth *through the Spirit* unto unfeigned love of the brethren, see that ye love one another with a pure heart fervently" (I Pet. 1:22). The soul can be purified, not the flesh. The soul can be converted, not the flesh. "It is the Spirit that giveth life; the flesh profiteth nothing. The words that I speak unto you, they are spirit, and they are life" (John 6:63). If we don't purify the flesh what do we do with it? **You can crucify the flesh.** "And they that are Christ's have crucified the flesh with the affections and lust" (Gal. 5:24). **You can mortify the flesh.** "Therefore, brethren, we are debtors, not to the flesh to live after the flesh, for if ye live after the flesh, ye shall die; but if ye, *through the Spirit,* do mortify the deeds of the body, ye shall live" (Ro. 8:12-13). You can reckon it dead. "Likewise, reckon ye also yourselves to be dead indeed unto sin, but alive unto God through Jesus Christ our Lord. Let not sin, therefore, reign in your mortal body that ye should obey it in its lust. Neither yield ye your members as instruments of unrighteousness unto sin, but yield yourselves unto God as those that are alive from the dead, and your members as instruments of righteousness unto God" (Rom. 6:11-13). Once again, the soul can be converted, but the flesh must go through the slow death of crucifixion.

In Luke 22:31, Jesus said these words to Peter just prior to going to the garden of Gethsemane on the night of his betrayal by Judas: "Simon, Simon, behold, Satan hath desired to have you, that he may sift you as wheat; but I have prayed for thee that your faith fail not. *And when thou art converted*, strengthen the brethren." Was Peter a child of God at the time Jesus said this to him? We know from Luke 5:8 that Peter had seen himself a sinful man. No man can be born again who has not first seen himself a sinner. "This is a faithful saying, and worthy of all acceptance, that Christ Jesus came into the world to save sinners, of whom I am chief" (I Tim. 1:15). We know that Christ had told him that he had been chosen. "Ye have not chosen me, but I have chosen you and ordained you that ye should go and bring forth fruit, and that your fruit should remain" (John 15:16). In Matthew 16:17-18: Peter, through the Spirit, had confessed that Jesus was the Christ, the Son of the living God, and Jesus said He would build His church upon Peter's confession. In Luke 10:20, Jesus had told Peter that his name was written down in heaven. Yes, Peter was born again, and as he grew in grace and the knowledge of the Lord Jesus, his soul would undergo changes—changes in the way he thought and felt, and thus, in the way he would behave.

Jesus instructed him to pass on what he learned so that it would strengthen the brethren.

Can someone have a converted soul and not be born again? Can someone undergo a change in his behavior, his attitude, and his values and never give God or the gospel so much as a thought? Many people have. I know of drunks who are sober and no longer drink, I know of thieves that no longer steal, of addicts that no longer use drugs. There are religious sects that employ biblical principles for family, finances, giving, serving, missionary work, and social involvement, and have no born-again experience. Lost and saved people alike benefit from living by biblical principles, but living like a Christian doesn't make one a Christian, no more than sounding like an engine makes you a car. It is possible to know the language of a Christian and not know the Lord. It's possible to convert to Christianity and not to Christ. Nicodemus himself was a man trying to live a spiritual life without the Spirit of God. "For what shall it profit a man, if he shall gain the whole world and lose his own soul? Or what shall a man give in exchange for his soul?" (Mark 8:36-37).

Can a man know if he is really born again? "Examine yourselves, whether you are in the faith; *prove yourselves.* Know ye not yourselves how Jesus Christ is in you, unless you are discredited?" (II Cor. 13:5). There could be many proofs listed in response to that question; I will only mention a few.

47

When the Spirit of God comes to reside in your body, He brings with Him genuine desires for the things of God, such as a desire for the word of God. "As newborn babes, desire the pure milk of the word, that ye may grow by it" (I Pet. 2:2). There will be a desire to obey the word of God (I Pet. 1:2). He brings a desire to grow in the grace and knowledge of God (II Pet. 3:18). You will experience true worship of God (John 4:24). Sometimes creation will cause you to spontaneously declare His glory (Ps. 19:1). You will sense His Spirit leading you in the way of godliness. "For as many as are led by the spirit of God, they are the sons of God" (Rom. 8:14). "He leadeth me in the paths of righteousness for his name's sake" (Ps. 23:3). You will experience comfort in times of trial. "I will not leave you comfortless; I will come to you" (John 14:18). The Holy Spirit will be your teacher. But the comforter, who is the Holy Spirit, whom the Father will send in my name, he shall teach you all things, and bring all things to your remembrance, whatever I have said unto you" (John 14:26). He will even reveal the deep things of God to you." But God hath revealed them unto us by his Spirit; for the Spirit searcheth all things, yea, the deep things of God" (I Cor. 2:10).

One may ask, "But how do I know it is God's Spirit producing these things in my life and not just my fleshly desires dressed up in religious clothing?" The best exam you can give yourself is simply this: honestly ask yourself, *"Who gets the glory?"* "Nevertheless, when he, the Spirit of truth, is come, He will guide you into all truth; for he shall not speak of himself, but whatever he shall hear, that shall he speak; and he will show you things to come. *He shall glorify me*; for he shall receive of mine and shall show it unto you" (John 16:13-14). "Let your light so shine before men, that they may see your good works, *and glorify your Father*, who is in heaven" (Matt. 5:16). "But *God forbid that I should glory*, except in the cross of our Lord Jesus Christ, by whom the world is crucified unto me, and I unto the world" (Gal. 6:14). "That no flesh should glory in His presence. But of Him are ye in Christ Jesus, who of God is made unto us wisdom, and righteousness, and sanctification, and redemption; That, according as it is written, he that glorieth, let him glory in the Lord" (I Cor. 1:29-31). "Whether, therefore, ye eat or ye drink or whatever ye do, do all to the glory of God" (I Cor. 10:31).

The conversion of my soul can expect opposition from the world and the devil, but most of all from the flesh. "For the flesh lusteth against the Spirit, and the Spirit against the flesh; and these two are contrary the one to the other, so that ye cannot do the things that ye would" (Gal. 5:17). If we, through the Spirit, obey the word of God, the fruit of the Spirit will be evident in our lives. "But the fruit of the Spirit is love, joy, peace, longsuffering, gentleness, goodness, faith, meekness, temperance, against such there is no law" (Gal. 5:22-23). If we allow the flesh to control our soul, the fruit of our lives will be similar to that of an unbeliever. When a person is filled with the Spirit (Eph. 5:18), the soul tells the body what to do. When a person is walking in the flesh, the flesh tells the soul what to do. If we walk in obedience to the Spirit, we won't fulfill the lust of the flesh (Gal. 5:17). If we cultivate spiritual things in our life, the soul will eventually go through a change. This change is called conversion.

> And besides this, giving all diligence, add to your faith virtue; and to virtue, knowledge; and to knowledge, self-control; and to self-control, patience; and to patience, godliness; and to godliness, brotherly kindness; and to brotherly kindness, love. For if these things be in you and abound, they shall make you that ye shall neither be barren nor unfruitful in the knowledge of our Lord Jesus Christ (II Pet. 1:5-8).

The soul will eventually undergo a change, or become converted to the ways of the new spiritual man (II Cor. 5:17).

A Spirit-controlled soul is a powerful thing, evidenced by perpetual thankfulness to God as well as reverent submission to Him, and to others. A flesh-controlled soul is also a powerful thing, along with help from the world and the devil, capable of performing unimaginable things that still live within the dim regions of a totally depraved heart. To my shame and regret, I have too often known the overwhelming power of a flesh-controlled soul. But, blessed be God, my spirit is becoming strong in the Lord, and by His grace, I am learning the ways of a Spirit-controlled soul. Many areas of my soul have experienced genuine conversion, where the old man and his ways have been put off and the new man which is after Christ has been put on. Yet there are still many areas of my soul where I feel vulnerable to the flesh and must acknowledge the need for further change.

Chapter 6:

Kingdom Living

Many people who think of the Kingdom of God think of it as something that is future tense only. They think only in terms of "when I die, I get to go to heaven." Though this is true, there is a present tense aspect of the kingdom of God that comes to life for those who are born again. This is what Jesus was making reference to in Matthew 6:10 when he prayed, "Thy kingdom come; Thy will be done on earth, as it is in heaven." In John 3:3, Jesus told Nicodemus that unless he was born again, he could not see the kingdom of God, present tense. But then two verses later Jesus told him that unless he was born of water and of the Spirit, he could not enter the kingdom of God, future tense. What is kingdom living, anyway? Simply said, kingdom living is acknowledging that Jesus Christ is the King of Kings and submitting to his sovereign authority in my daily life. In John 18:37, Pilate asked Jesus if he were a king. Jesus said, "To this end was I born, for this cause came I into the world, that I should bear witness unto the truth." A major part of present-tense kingdom living is bearing witness of the truth, living in such a manner that it becomes obvious to me and to others that someone greater than me is calling the shots in my life. No matter what other kingdoms make demands of me, His kingdom has top priority, and I bow to his authority in my life above all others.

WORLD KINGDOMS

What about world kingdoms? "The devil took Jesus up into an exceedingly high mountain, and showed him the kingdoms of this world, and the glory of them, and saith unto him, all these will I give unto thee if thou wilt fall down and worship me. Then Jesus said unto him, be gone, Satan; for it is written, thou shalt worship the Lord thy God, and him only shalt thou serve" (Matt. 4:8-10). God had already determined the four kingdoms of this world and had revealed them in his word through the prophet Daniel. History confirms these world kingdoms as follows: the Babylonian Kingdom, The Medeo-Persian Kingdom, Greece, and Rome. Though other nations have attempted world dominance, all have failed, and we continue to live under the influence of the fourth world power, which will conclude catastrophically at the return of the Lord Jesus and the coming of his Kingdom to earth. As citizens of the Kingdom of God, we are to obey our government in all good conscience and be good citizens, knowing that God has ordained government for our good (Rom. 13:1-7). Another aspect of understanding kingdom living is knowing that God, the King of Kings, is the one who both removes earthly kings and sets them up (Dan. 2;21).

Kingdom Of Darkness

Beware of the Kingdom of Darkness! In Ephesians 2:2, Satan is called the prince of the power of the air, the spirit that now works in the sons of disobedience. "Put on the whole armor of God, that you may be able to stand against the wiles of the devil. For we wrestle not against flesh and blood but against principalities, against powers, against the rulers of the darkness of this world, against spiritual wickedness in high places" (Eph. 6:11-12). Revelation 16:10 says that Satan's kingdom is full of darkness. Darkness is a metaphor referring to unimaginable wickedness and evil, and the violent hatred of God and his people. I Peter 5:8-9 warns us to "Be sober, be vigilant, because your adversary, the devil, like a roaring lion walks about seeking whom he may devour; whom resist steadfast in the faith, knowing that the same afflictions are accomplished in your brethren that are in the world." People who know the Lord know what it is to be opposed by Satan, and they also know what it is to be delivered from the dominion of darkness and know they have been translated into the kingdom of God's dear Son (Col. 1:13). Those people born of the Spirit of God have experienced the reality of kingdoms in conflict, the kingdom of darkness and the kingdom of light. In times of conflict with Satan, it's comforting to know that greater is he that is in us than he that is in the world (I John 4:4).

Religious Kingdoms

Beware of religious kingdoms! Nicodemus was caught up in a religious kingdom that was built upon the scriptures. Though it seemed built upon the scriptures, the kingdom he found himself in with so many of his fellow law keepers had a form of godliness, but denied it's power. He would be quick to defend his doctrine and have scripture to support his argument. He could strain at a gnat and swallow a camel as quick as any Pharisee. The Apostle Paul gave good advice to Timothy when he said, "O Timothy, keep that which is committed to thy trust, avoiding profane and vain babblings, and oppositions of knowledge falsely so called, which some, professing, have erred from the truth concerning the faith. Grace be with thee" (I Tim.

6:20-21). Paul gave similar advice to Titus in verse 1:14, "Not giving heed to Jewish fables, and commandments of men that turn from the truth." and 3:9, "But avoid foolish questions and genealogies, and contentions, and strivings about the law; for they are unprofitable and vain." A man's denominational tag isn't worth a biscuit. I heard it said, "Your denominational tag is either going to fall off on the way to heaven or burn off on the way to hell." "But foolish and unlearned questions avoid, knowing that they breed strifes. And the servant of the Lord must not strive, but be gentle unto all men, apt to teach, patient, in meekness instructing those that oppose him, if God perhaps will give them repentance to the acknowledging of the truth (II Tim. 2:23-25)." If the Lord Jesus is King of your life, you will be able to see that he would want you to walk worthy of the vocation to which you were called, with all lowliness and meekness, with longsuffering, forbearing one another in love, endeavoring to keep the unity of the Spirit in the bond of peace. When truly born-again people become mean with each other and argue and separate over some system of theology that for the most part contains some measure of obscurity, we are guilty of building a religious kingdom of whom Jesus is not the king.

Beware Of Personal Kingdoms

And he spoke a parable unto them, saying, the ground of a certain rich man brought forth plentifully. And he thought within himself saying, What shall I do, because I have no place to bestow my crops? And he said, this will I do: I will pull down my barns and build greater; and there will I bestow all my crops and my goods, and I will say to my soul, Soul thou hast much goods laid up for many years; take thine ease. Eat, drink, and be merry. But God said unto him, Thou fool, this night thy soul shall be required of thee; then whose shall those things be, which thou hast provided? So is he that layeth up treasure for himself, and is not rich toward God (Luke 12:16-21).

"With what difficulty shall they that have riches enter into the kingdom of God! For it is easier for a camel to go through a needle's eye, than for a rich man to enter the kingdom of God" (Luke 18:24-25). Being born again allows a man to experience or see kingdom living in this life. This is the only way we can lay up treasure in heaven. Kingdom living is easier to preach than it is to live, and for many, personal kingdoms come down hard. Getting focused on eternity is one thing; staying focused is quite another.

The kingdom of God and the will of God are inseparable. Jesus said, "Thy kingdom come; thy will be done, on earth as it is in heaven" (Matt. 6:10). Jesus personified kingdom living when he prayed in the garden of Gethsemane, "Father, all things are possible unto thee, let this cup pass from me, nevertheless, *not my will but thine be done*" (Matt. 26:39). "Lo, I come (in the volume of the book it is written of me), to do thy will O God" (Heb. 10:7). Kingdom living is doing the will of the King. When the Apostle Paul met the Lord Jesus on the Damascus road and received his spiritual sight, his first response was to ask, "What wilt thou have me to do?" The moment he was born again, he knew it, but it took some time before he knew how to best go about it. Many sincere believers want to know God's will for their lives and desire to live for his kingdom, but don't know where to begin. Learning to do the obvious will of God will oftentimes be the means God uses in revealing the details of his deeper will.

Doing The Known Will Of God As Found In Scripture

Apart from the word of God, we have no sure understanding of the will of God. Here are five scriptures that tell us the known will of God.

1. **"In everything give thanks** for this is the will of God in Christ Jesus concerning you" (I Thess. 5:18). Cultivating an attitude of thankfulness is one of the greatest things a child of God can do. It has the capacity to cleanse him of greed and selfishness like no other exercise he can do. "Every good gift and every perfect gift is from above, and cometh down from the father of lights, with whom there is no variableness, neither shadow of turning" (James 1:17). Never let a day pass that you do not thank God for your salvation, the greatest gift you could ever receive. Be thankful for all that went into making it possible for you to become a child of God. Thank God for conviction of sin, for repentance, and mercy, and grace, and faith, for the word of the gospel and the person who cared enough to tell you. But don't just stop with thanking him for the good things that come into your life; in everything give thanks, even in the difficult things that come into your life. Most of us are drawn closer to God through hard times than in times of ease. Remember to give thanks in all things.

Give thanks in the things you normally take for granted. I learned this from a godly old man while leaving a restroom. I heard him say in a low tone, "Thank you." We were the only two in the men's room, and I knew I was not being thanked. I asked him what he had said thanks for, and he told me he was eighty-eight years old and thankful he had never had any prostate or urinary problems. A few years later, I had some serious medical problems in that area, and after the doctors fixed the problem, I have been consciously thankful ever since. Most of us aren't thankful enough when we are well.

2. **Be filled with the Spirit.** Ephesians 5:15-18 sets the stage perfectly for the second known will of God: "See then that ye walk circumspectly, not as fools but as wise, redeeming the time because the days are evil. Wherefore, be not unwise, but understanding what the will of the Lord is. And be not drunk with wine, in which is excess, but be filled with the Spirit." Volumes of books have been written on what it means to be filled with the Spirit and how to be filled with the Spirit. Without a doubt, this brief paragraph won't cover it all, but maybe something will be said to help us get started in that direction. Be careful in how you walk. Live your life with as much precision and accuracy towards righteousness as you can (Phil. 1:11). Always deal thoroughly with you own sin. Don't look for the splinter in someone else's eye and overlook the beam that's in your own. The days are evil—you can count on it, so acknowledge God in prayer in all your ways, and he will direct your paths. Be careful not to do the sin of Ananias and Sapphira and keep back part of your life for yourself (Acts 5:3). The condition of being filled with the Spirit is something we must give constant attention to and is truly the secret to Kingdom living.

Prayer has become the greatest asset in attempting to live a Spirit-filled life. I have tried to incorporate Proverbs 3:6, "In all thy ways acknowledge him, and he will direct thy paths." The difference short prayers have made in the directing of my soul is one of the greatest blessings of my spiritual journey. There is a God in heaven who hears our prayers, restores our souls, and leads us in the paths of righteousness (Ps. 23:3).

3. **Present your body a living sacrifice.** "I beseech you therefore, brethren, by the mercies of God, that you present your bodies a living sacrifice, holy, acceptable unto God, which is your reasonable service. And be not conformed to this world, but be ye transformed by the renewing of your mind, that ye may prove what is that good, and acceptable, and perfect will of God" (Rom. 12:1-2). I Corinthians 6:19-20: "What? Know ye not that your body is the temple of the Holy Spirit, who is in you, whom ye have of God, and ye are not your own? For ye are bought with a price; therefore glorify God in your body and in your spirit which are God's" (I Cor. 6:19-20). Consciously give God your eyes, which means, you just can't look at any old thing you want to look at. Your eyes now belong to God. Jesus said if a man looks on a woman to lust after her, he has committed adultery with her already in his heart. Consciously give your feet to God, which means you just can't go any old place you want to go. Give your ears to God, which means you can't listen to any old thing you want to. Your ears are not garbage buckets for gossip or for any sounds that might turn your heart away from God. The tongue is also dangerous thing. James 3 calls the tongue a world

of iniquity and says that it is set on fire of hell and can destroy the whole course of nature. No man can tame it by himself; only God can help him with it. Consciously take every member of your anatomy and present it to God for service in his Kingdom. "Neither yield ye your members as instruments of unrighteousness unto sin, but yield yourselves unto God as those that are alive from the dead, and your members as instruments of righteousness unto God" (Rom. 6:13).

4. **Be morally pure.** "For this is the will of God, even your sanctification, that you should abstain from fornication; that every one of you should know how to possess his vessel in sanctification and honor, not in the lust of sensuality, even as the heathen who know not God" (I Thess. 4:3-5). Paul told Timothy in his first letter to him (chapter 5, verse 22) to keep himself pure. Keeping oneself morally pure is no small task. Our sexuality is a God-created thing, yet the sin that lives within us and the world we live in and the devil himself all want us to use this God-created desire in a God-forbidden way. I am sobered when I think that the strongest man that ever lived (Samson), the bravest man that ever lived (David), and the wisest man that ever lived (Solomon), as well as Judah, from whose family line the Lord Jesus would eventually come, were all defeated in this area of the will of God. As is true in all areas of the will of God, he will never command us to do anything that he will not enable us to accomplish. The divine enabling power of God is

called grace and is recorded for us in many places. "And God is able to make all grace abound toward you that ye, always with all sufficiency in all things, may abound unto every good work" (II Cor. 9:8). "That as sin has reigned unto death, even so might grace reign through righteousness unto eternal life by Jesus Christ our Lord" (Rom. 5:21). The power of God to overcome sin is found in grace, and grace is found when we come boldly to the throne of grace and ask for mercy and cleansing. "Purge me with hyssop, and I shall be clean; wash me, and I shall be whiter than snow" (Ps. 51:7). "If we confess our sins, he is faithful and just to forgive us our sins and to cleanse us from all unrighteousness" (I John 1:9). Ask then for grace to help in time of need, when the temptation is at its worst, and you will find him faithful to supply his grace (Heb. 4:16). As you experience victory, you will become stronger and stronger in the Lord and the power of his might. Freedom from this sin is something that needs maintenance; keep thyself pure.

5. **The will of God may include suffering.** "Wherefore, let them who suffer according to the will of God, commit the keeping of their souls to him in well-doing, as unto a faithful Creator" I Pet. 4:19). We must keep in mind that, even though we are born again and our citizenship is in heaven, we remain here on earth, where we are exposed to the consequences of our sin-cursed earth like everyone else. Being born again does

not make us immune to sickness and disease. Being a Christian doesn't mean you never have a trial or a trouble or experience a financial setback. In John 16:33: Jesus said, "In the world ye shall have tribulation: but be of good cheer; I have overcome the world." "For whatever is born of God overcometh the world; and this is the victory that overcometh the world, even our faith" (I John 5:4). "For the kingdom of God is not food and drink, but righteousness, and peace and joy in the Holy Spirit" (Rom. 14:17). The kingdom of God is not having everyone hear the gospel of the kingdom and receive it with open arms or love the messenger that brings it. It may be having people revile you and say all manner of evil against you falsely for the sake of the Lord. It may involve physical maladies from an automobile accident or a simple surgery gone wrong. It may involve the loss of some of the most important people in your life. A friend may betray you, or your spiritual mentor may fail you. A list of situations could go on and on, but the kingdom of God is not having everything go my comfortable way. True kingdom living is the righteousness, peace, and joy that the Holy Spirit brings. The Holy Spirit has assured me that my righteousness is the perfect righteousness of Jesus imputed to me at my new birth, and no amount of suffering can take that away from me. My peace and my joy are rooted in this great truth, and they remain regardless of the circumstances of this life.

Chapter 7:

Eternity

No word has influenced my life more than the word *eternity*. It stands in a class all by itself, and hands down, it is my favorite word. The concept is incomprehensible, and so is the God whom it attempts to describe. The God of the Bible has no circumference; he is from everlasting to everlasting. God is eternal. "For thus saith the high and lofty One who inhabiteth eternity, whose name is Holy: I dwell in the high and holy place, with him also who is of a contrite and humble spirit, to revive the spirit of the humble, and to revive the heart of the contrite ones" (Isa. 57:15). I am humbled at the thought of the eternal God creating man in his likeness—not his exactness, but his likeness. God is a spirit. "God is a Spirit; and they that worship him must worship him in spirit and in truth" (John 4:24). At creation, God put an eternal spirit in man, like himself. The spirit of man would now live for eternity. The devil tempted man and told him to do the only thing that God had commanded him not to do: eat of the forbidden fruit. Satan told Eve that if she would eat, she should be exactly like the God who created her. Eve was deceived when she believed the lie, and now Adam had to make a choice. He made the wrong one; and sin came into the world. The effect of Adam's sin would be felt by every succeeding generation.

This scene had been played out once before, when God created angels and they had sinned. "For if God spared not the angels that sinned, but cast them down to hell, and delivered them into chains of darkness, to be reserved unto judgment..." (II Pet. 2:4). At this time, God prepared a place of eternal judgment for the devil and his angels. "And the angels who kept not their first estate, but left their own habitation, he hath reserved in everlasting chains under darkness unto the judgment of the great day" (Jude 6). Man, who was created for fellowship with God in heaven, because of Adam's sin, now may have to spend eternity in Hell separated from the God who gave him his life. When the judgment of the great day of the Lord arrives, "the King [shall] say unto them on the right hand, Come ye blessed of my Father, inherit the kingdom prepared for you before the foundation of the world" (Matt. 25:34). "Then shall he say also unto them on the left hand, Depart from me, ye cursed, into everlasting fire, prepared for the devil and his angels" (Matt. 25:41). This is where the word *eternity* gets as serious as the grave. What if there were no word from God on how to know my eternal destiny? What if God had been silent on all he has done to make a way of salvation and eternal life? My plea to all who are reading is, hear the word of the Lord and believe, and God will forgive your sins and give you His Holy Spirit.

"But these are written, that ye might believe that Jesus is the Christ, the Son of God; and that believing ye might have life through his name" (John 20:31). This kind of believing is not just a nod of the head to believing there is a God. "Thou believest that there is one God; thou doest well. The demons also believe, and tremble" (James 2:19). This is not just believing in good theology. Oh, good theology is essential, but without true faith, it is immaterial. "Now faith is the substance of things hoped for, the evidence of things not seen" (Heb. 11:1). If the Spirit of God is convicting you of sin and leading you to repentance, it is your moment of grace; turn to God in faith, call out to Him in prayer, ask God to have mercy on you and to forgive your sin. In the faith God gives you at that moment, confess the Lord Jesus Christ as your only hope of eternal life. Ask God to come into your life and be your Savior and Lord.

What God has promised, he will do; his word is unbreakable. In John 10:27-29: Jesus said, "my sheep hear my voice, and I know them, and they follow me. And I give unto them eternal life; and they shall never perish, neither shall any man pluck them out of my hand. My Father who gave them to me is greater than all, and no man is able to pluck them out of my Father's hand." "For the wages of sin is death, but the gift of God is eternal life through Jesus Christ our Lord" (Rom. 6:23). Salvation is a gift freely given to those who believe. "Being justified freely by his grace through the redemption that is in Christ Jesus" (Rom. 3:24). "Wherefore, as the Holy Spirit saith, Today if ye will hear his voice, harden not your hearts" (Heb. 3:7-8).

Jesus made his invitations very simple: If you are thirsty, come and drink (John 7:37). No physical thirst was ever quenched by the water remaining in the glass. The glass of water must be picked up and drunk in. No thirst of a man's soul has ever been quenched until he drinks of the water that God gives him. The living water is the Lord Jesus Christ, and once you take him in, he will be in you a well of water springing up into life everlasting, and you will never thirst again (John 4:14). This is the first and most important step in the journey of faith. Ask the almighty God to have mercy on your soul, to forgive your sins and come into your life.

> Just a field hand,
> Your servant for Jesus' sake,
>
> Tom Harmon

CPSIA information can be obtained at www.ICGtesting.com
Printed in the USA
BVOW06s1427041013

332881BV00001B/1/P

9 781609 200152